POP PIANO HITS

SIMPLE ARRANGEMENTS FOR STUDENTS

Hello, Better When I'm Dancin' & More Hot Singles

ISBN 978-1-4950-5814-1

HAL•LEONARD®
CORPORATION

7777 W. BLUEMOUND RD. P.O. BOX 13819 MILWAUKEE, WI 53213

Visit Hal Leonard Online at
www.halleonard.com

Contents

BURNING HOUSE

Words and Music by JEFF BHASKER,
TYLER SAM JOHNSON and CAMARON OCHS

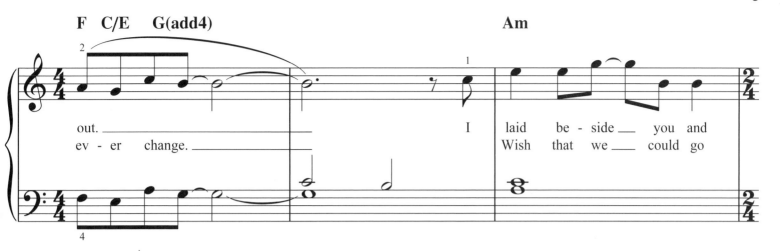

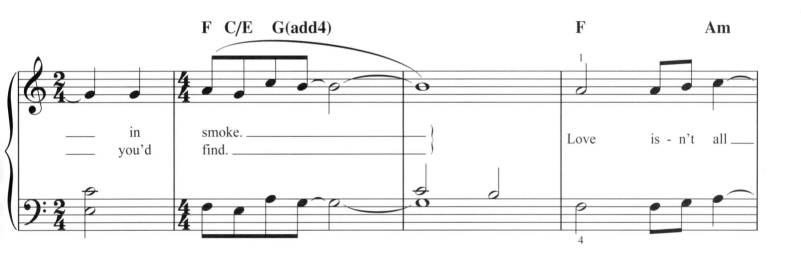

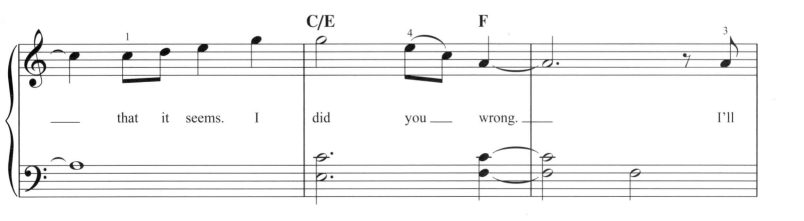

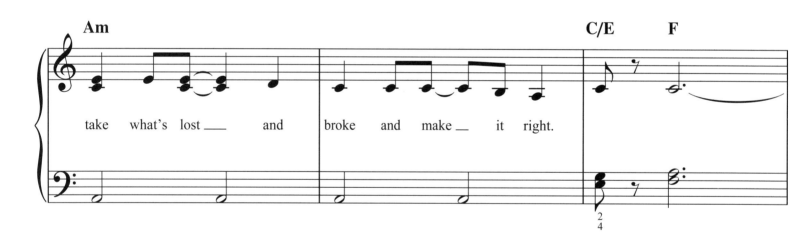

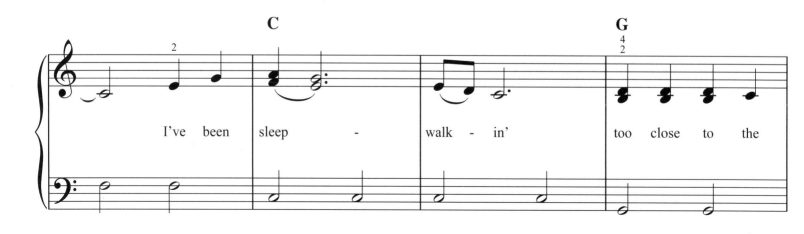

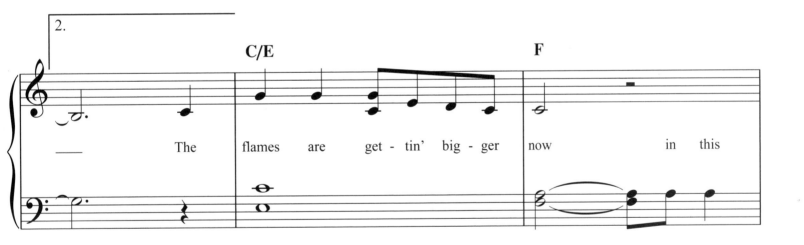

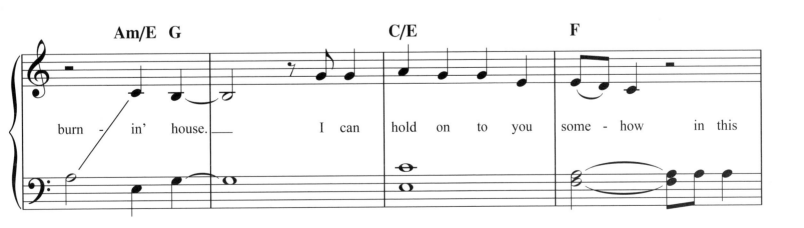

Am/E   G   C/E

burn - in' house.___   Oh, and   I don't wan - na

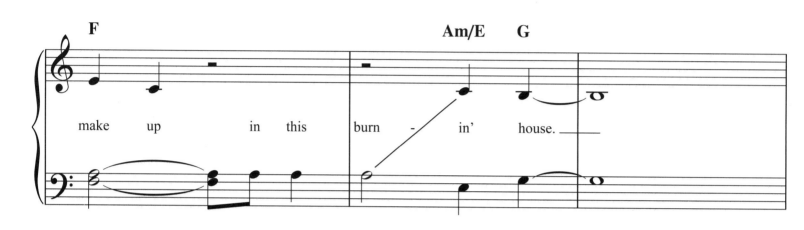

F   Am/E   G

make up   in this   burn - in'   house.___

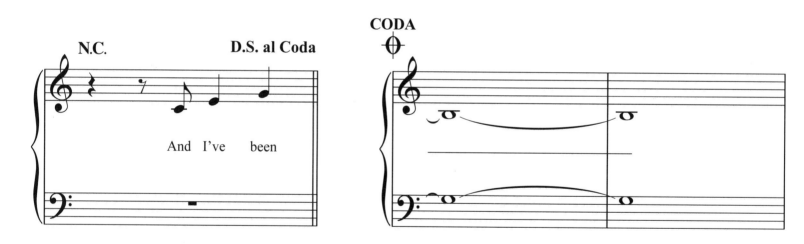

N.C.   D.S. al Coda   CODA

And I've been

C   Fmaj7   F   G

mp

BETTER WHEN I'M DANCIN'

from THE PEANUTS MOVIE

Words and Music by MEGHAN TRAINOR
and THADDEUS DIXON

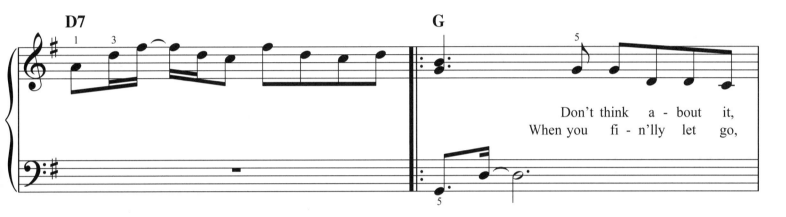

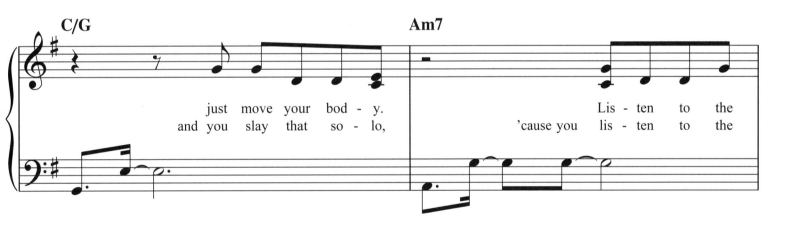

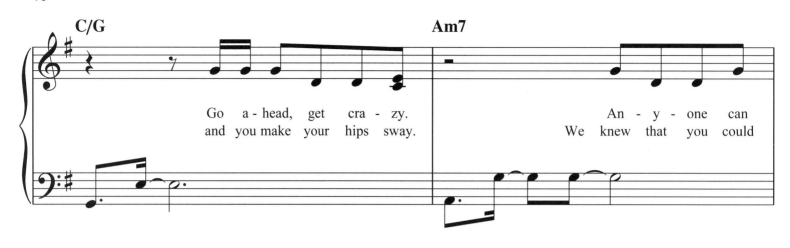

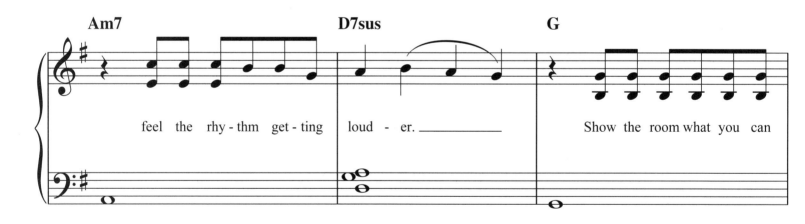

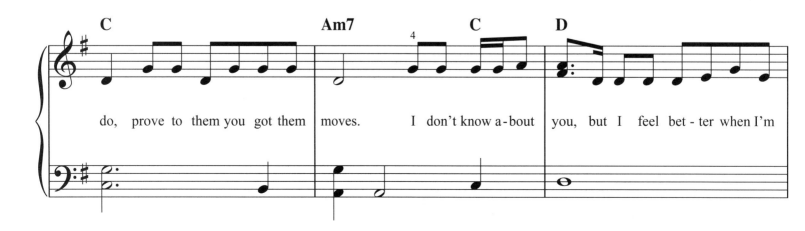

dan - cin', yeah, yeah. ___ I'm bet - ter when I'm dan - cin', yeah, yeah. ___

___ And we __ can do this to - geth - er. I bet __ you feel bet - ter when you're

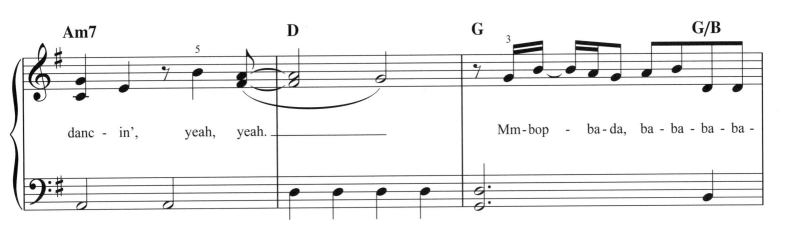

dan - cin', yeah, yeah. ___ Mm - bop - ba - da, ba - ba - ba - ba -

da - da, la - la - la - la - da - da, la - la - la - la - da - da, ___ bop - ba - da - da.

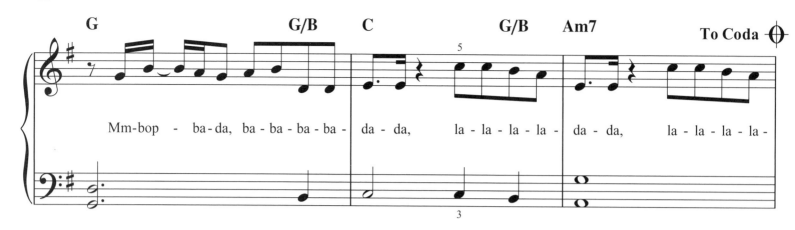

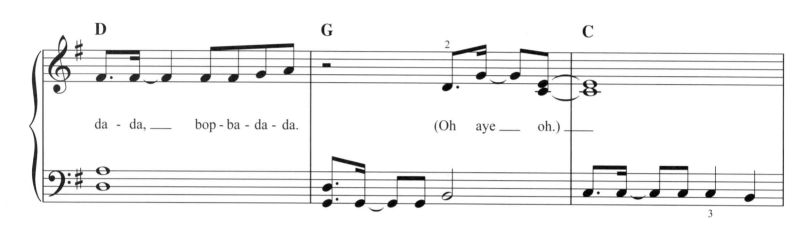

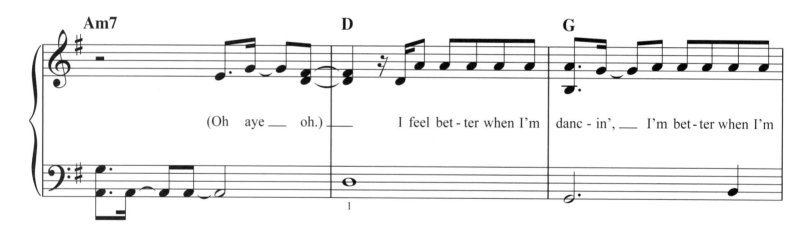

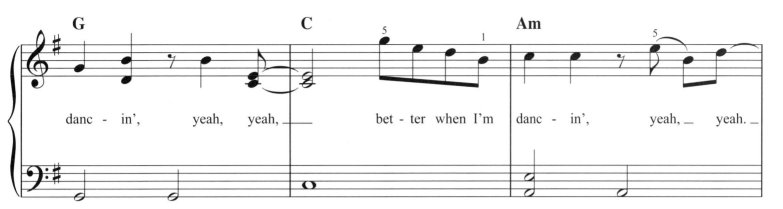

danc - in',   yeah,   yeah, ____   bet - ter when I'm   danc - in',   yeah, __   yeah. __

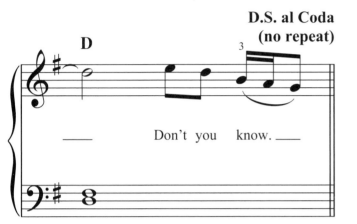

__   Don't you   know. __   da - da,   I feel bet - ter when I'm

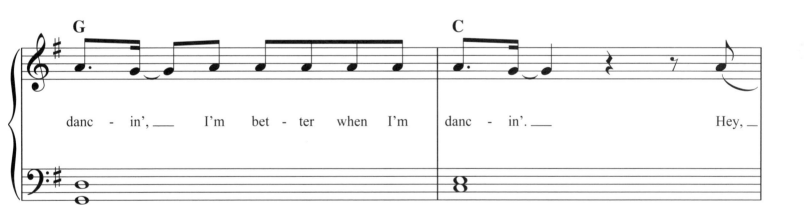

danc - in', __   I'm bet - ter   when   I'm   danc - in'. __   Hey, __

__   feel bet - ter when I'm...   yeah, __   yeah. __

DRAG ME DOWN

Words and Music by JOHN HENRY RYAN,
JAMIE SCOTT and JULIAN BUNETTA

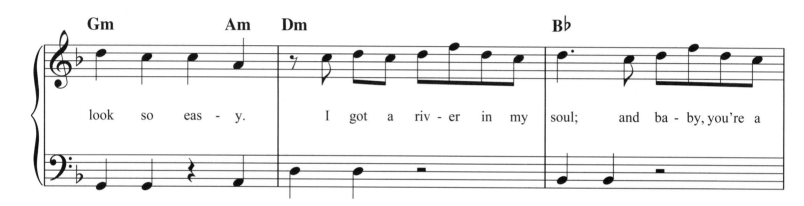

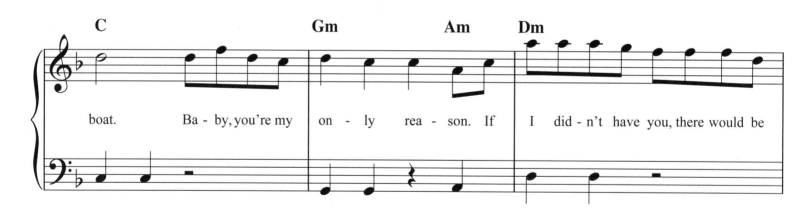

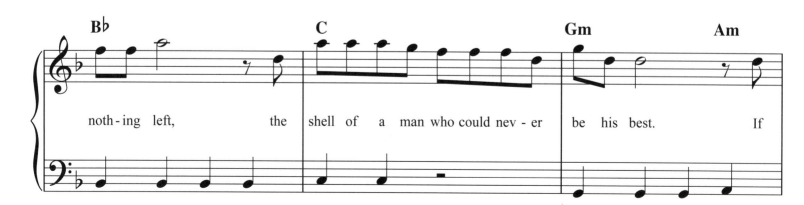

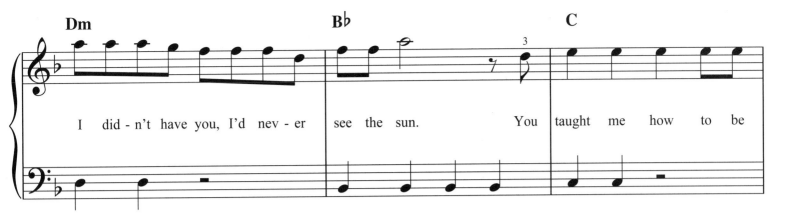

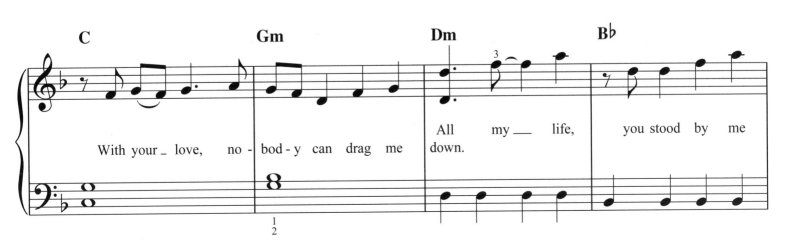

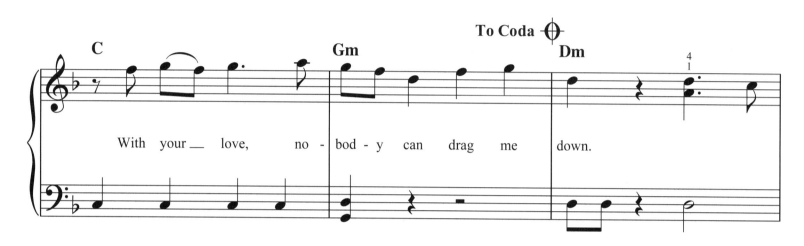

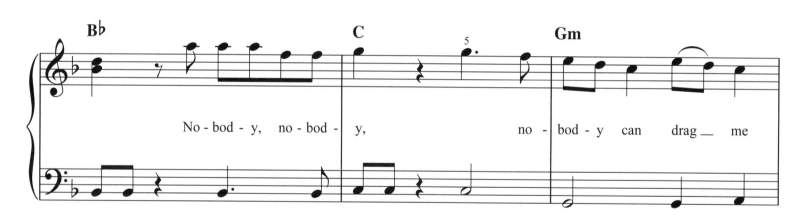

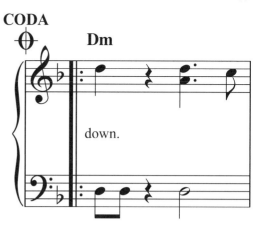

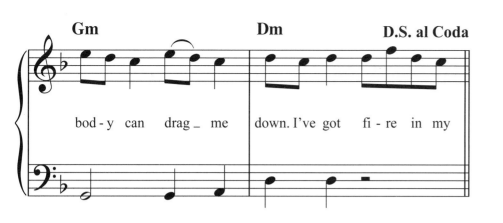

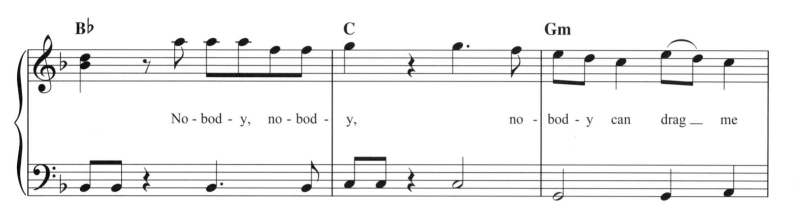

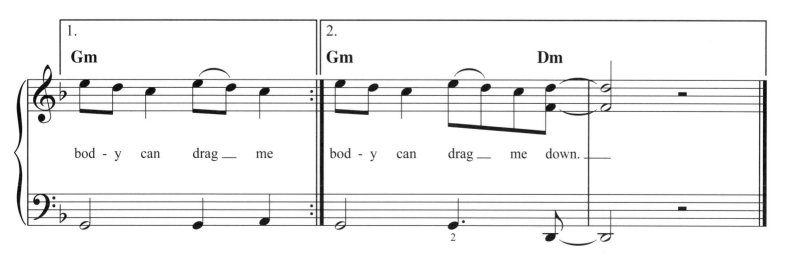

HELLO

Words and Music by ADELE ADKINS
and GREG KURSTIN

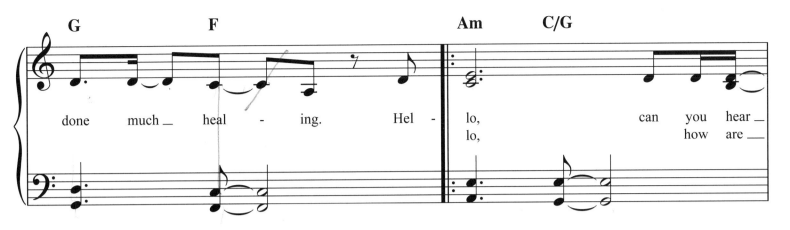

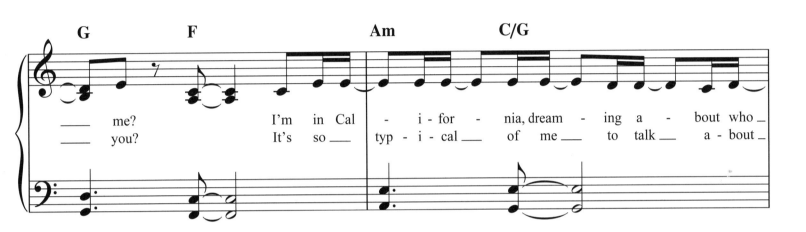

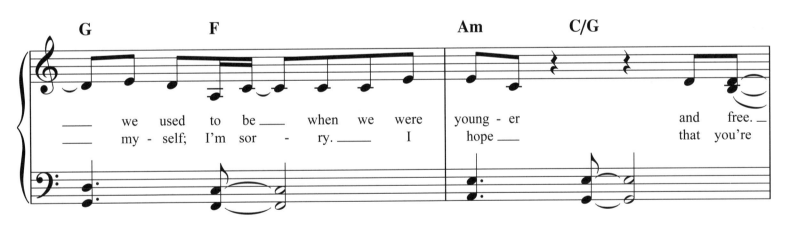

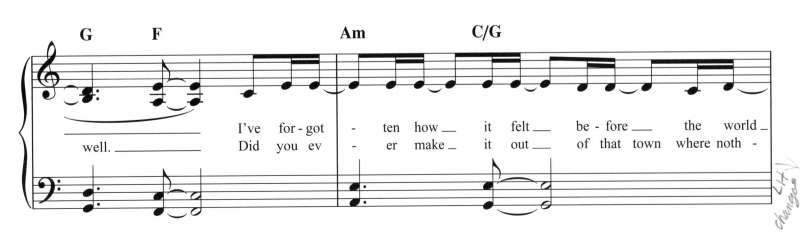

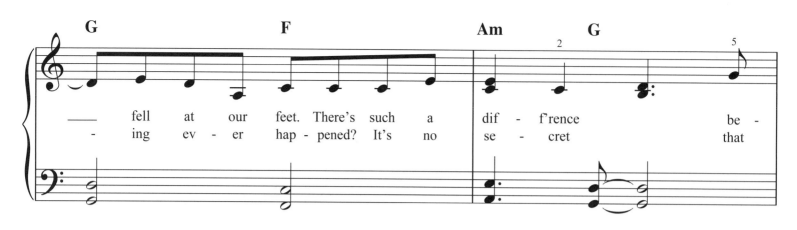

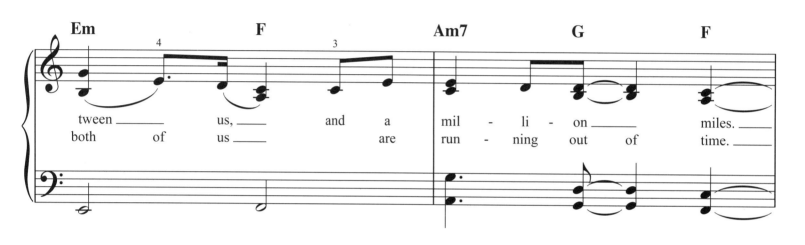

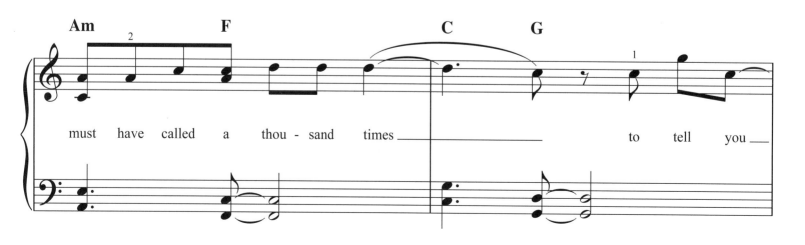

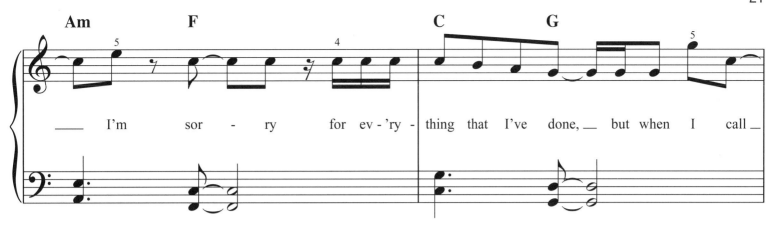

I'm sor - ry for ev -'ry - thing that I've done, __ but when I call __

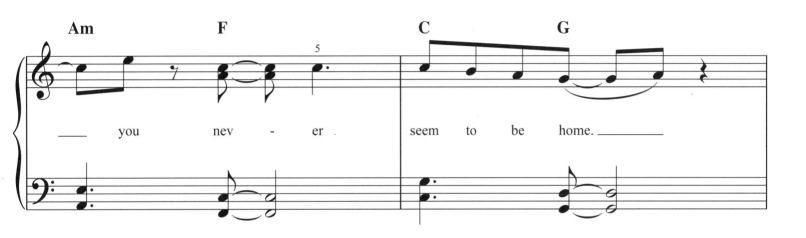

__ you nev - er __ seem to be home. _____

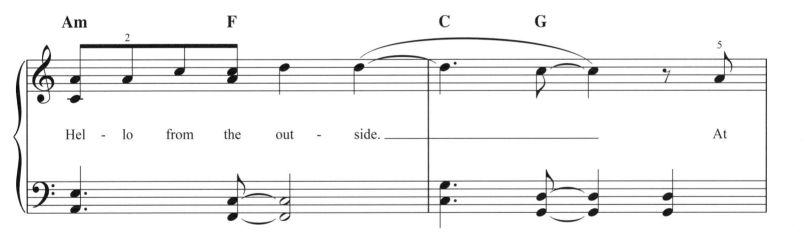

Hel - lo from the out - side. _____ At

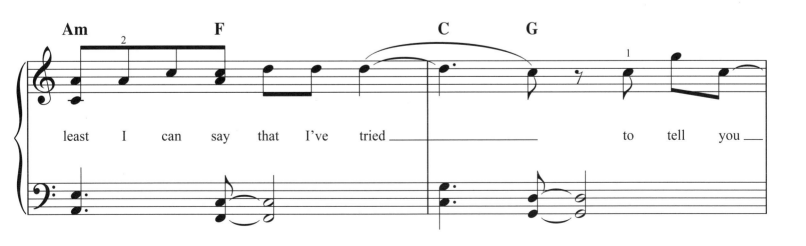

least I can say that I've tried _____ to tell you __

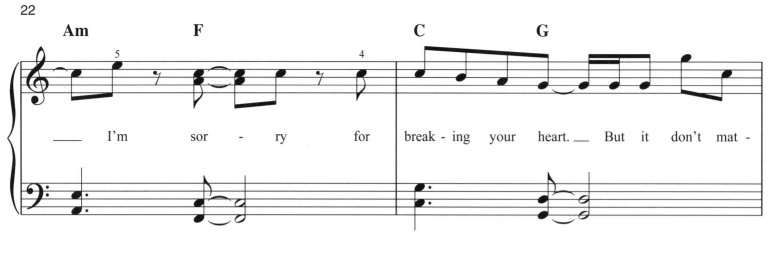

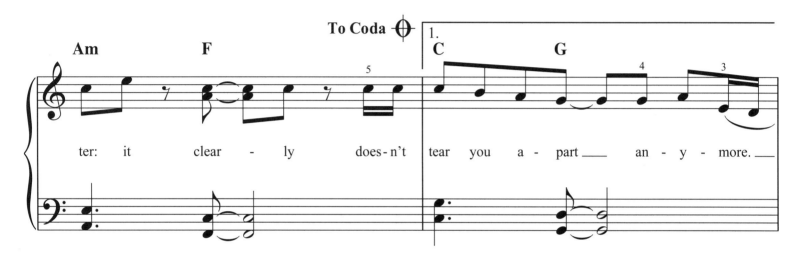

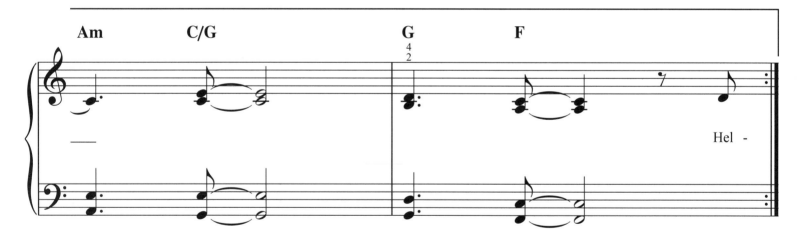

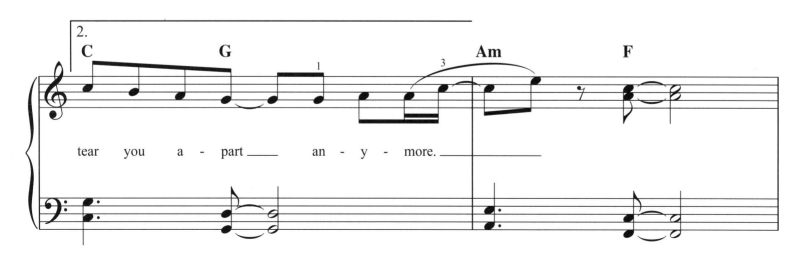

SHE USED TO BE MINE
from WAITRESS THE MUSICAL

Words and Music by
SARA BAREILLES

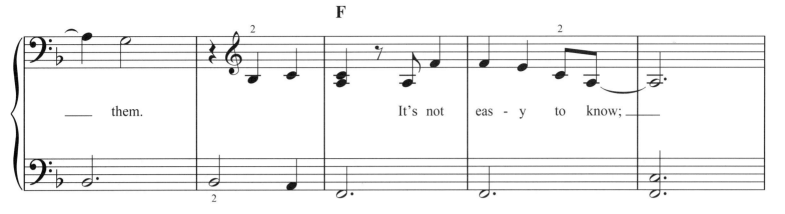

them.   It's not   eas - y   to   know; ___

I'm   not   an - y - thing   like   I   used   to   be, ___   al - though   it's   true, ___

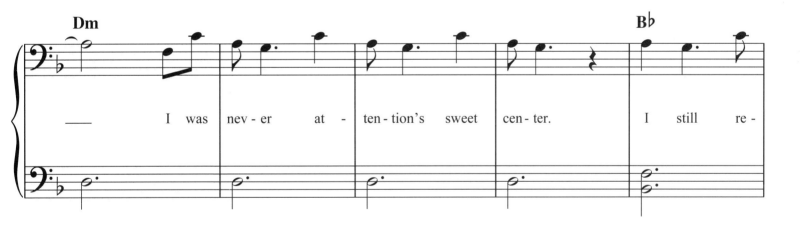

___   I   was   nev - er   at - ten - tion's   sweet   cen - ter.   I   still   re -

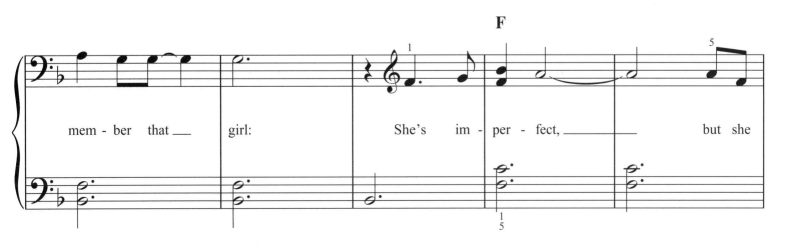

mem - ber   that ___   girl: She's   im - per - fect, _____   but   she

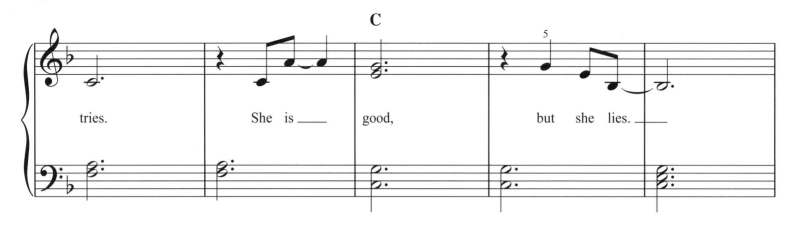

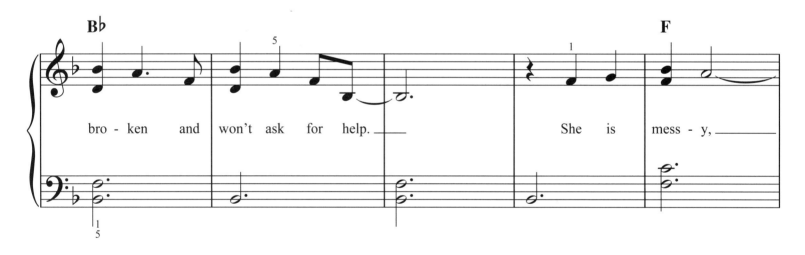

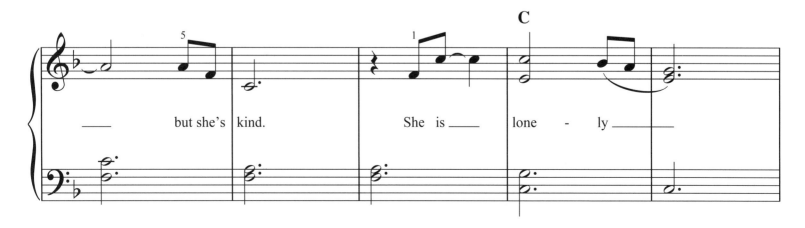

Dm

most of the time. ____ She is all of this, ___ mixed up and

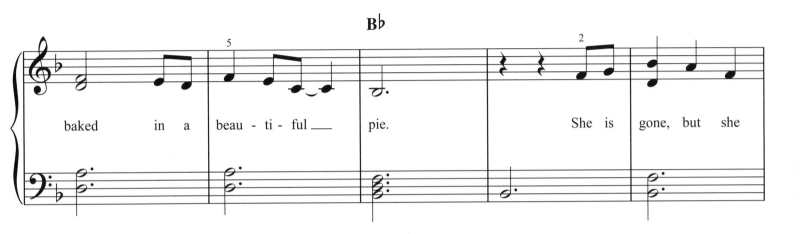

B♭

baked in a beau - ti - ful ___ pie. She is gone, but she

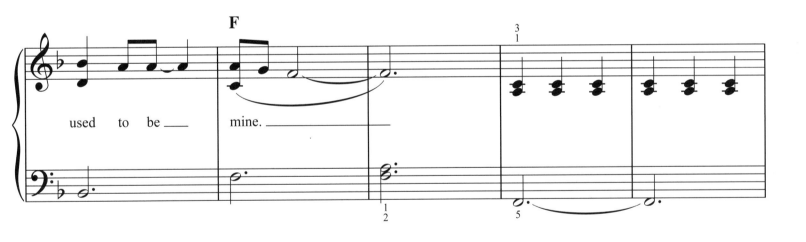

F

used to be ___ mine.

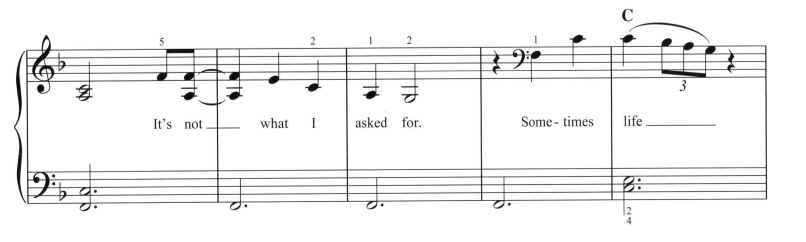

C

It's not ___ what I asked for. Some - times life ____

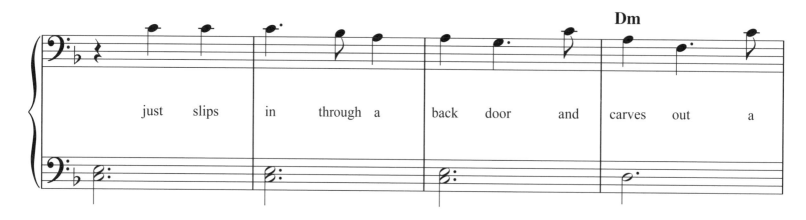

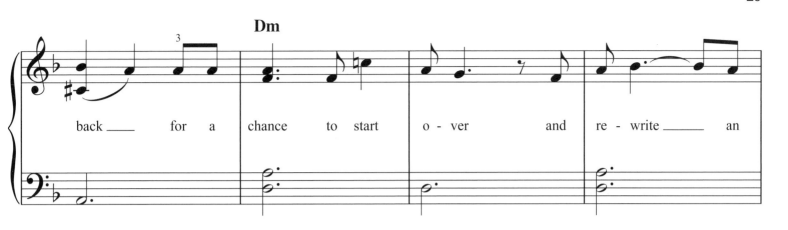

back _____ for a chance to start o - ver and re - write _____ an

end - ing or two for the girl that I knew, who'd be

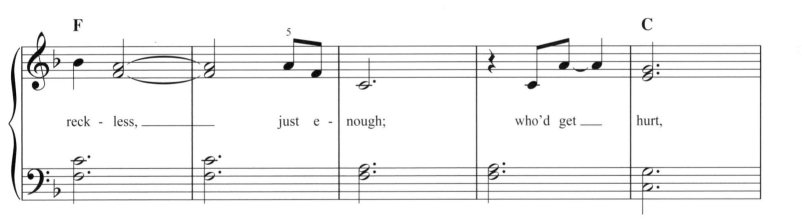

reck - less, _____ just e - nough; who'd get ___ hurt,

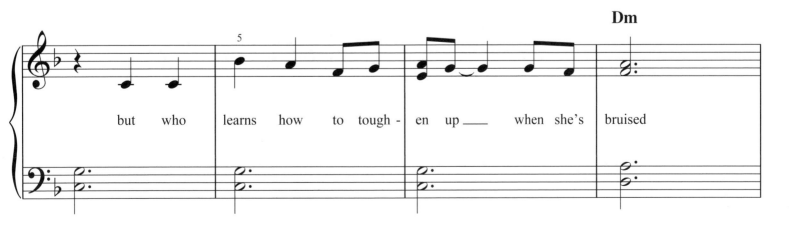

but who learns how to tough - en up ___ when she's bruised

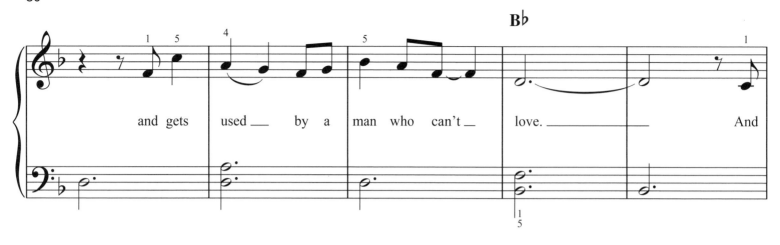

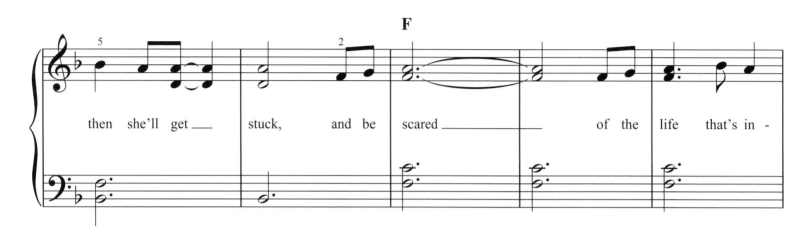

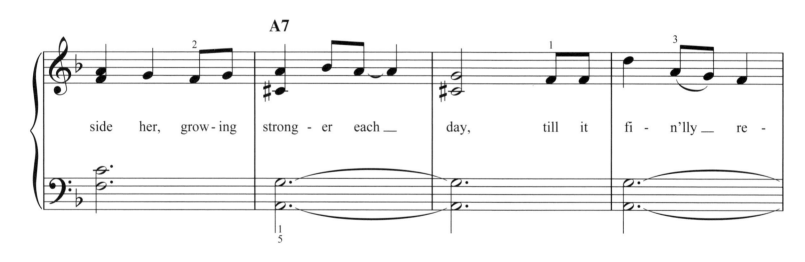

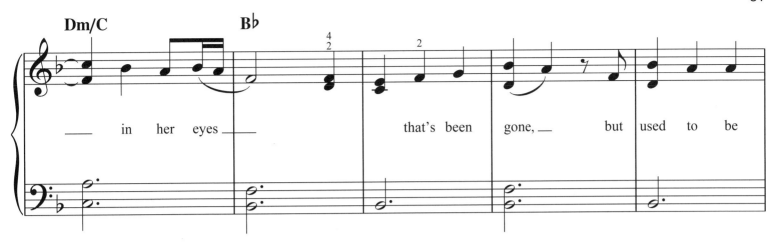

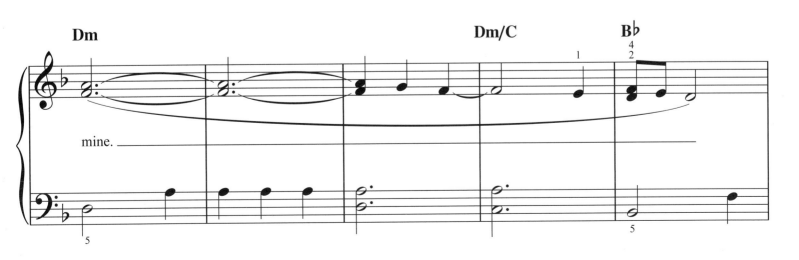

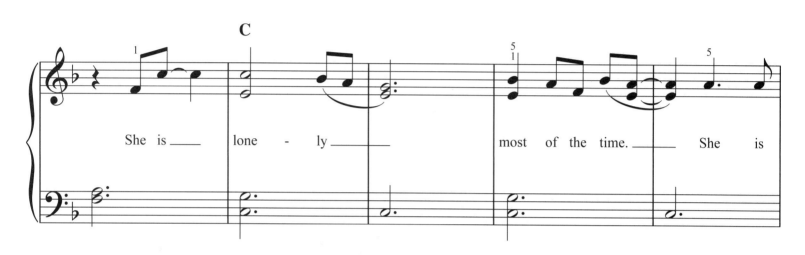

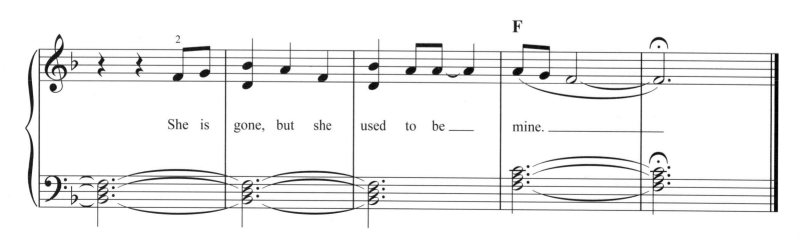